W9-ADJ-360

guide to
Segovia

Text, photographs, design, lay-out and printing, entirely created by the technical department of EDITORIAL ESCUDO DE ORO, S.A.

Rights of total or partial reproduction and translation reserved.

2nd Edition

I.S.B.N. 84-378-1830-3

Dep. Legal B. 37070-2000

HOW TO USE THIS GUIDE

Segovia is of the richest Spanish provinces in terms of monuments and variety of scenery. This guide aims to help visitors travel around the province with greater ease, offering in a pleasant way the basic information travellers need to enjoy the singular natural beauties, art and gastronomy of the province.

To this end we suggest seven itineraries (each identified by its own colour) which visitors will find useful as they find out more about the delights of this miniature paradise. Always taking Segovia capital as the starting-point and final destination, and using that city as a point of reference, all the routes are designed to be completed in a day whilst allowing sufficient time to fully appreciate each recommended sight.

Moreover, the reader will find at the end of this guide a map of the province showing each itinerary, and another of Segovia capital at the beginning of the first route to help visitors find their way around the streets of the city.

We also include, following on from this description of how to use the guide several introductory pages providing background to the history, art, gastronomy and folklore of Segovia.

To get to know Segovia and its province, to become immersed in it and understand its life, its magic, just let yourself wander around its tiny streets, admiring its monuments, lose yourself in its landscapes. All this and much more makes Segovia an unforgettable destination.

HAVE A GOOD TRIP!

HISTORICAL INTRODUCTION

The innumerable architectural and artistic vestiges to be found in the province of Segovia reveal its enormous importance in the cultural history of Spain.

There are in the province Neolithic settlements around the River Duratón between Sepúlveda and the Burguillo reservoir, as well as graffiti on the rocks in the rural district of Santa María La Real de Nieva and Carbonero el Mayor. Dating to the Bronze Age are necropolises and settlements in Torreiglesias, Prádena, Armuña, Pedraza and Villaseca. The Celtiberian culture also occupied these settlements, and interesting remains from that culture have been found in the vicinity.

The Romanisation of the province was not intense, but did leave such exceptional vestiges as the famous Aqueduct in Segovia city, used since the Reconquest as its heraldic emblem. Coca was the childhood home of Trajan, whilst Roman remains have also been found in Aguilafuente, Madrona and Paradinas.

The Visigoth period saw the beginning of decline in the province, despite the fact that Segovia was episcopal see and the excellent remains of Visigoth necropolises in Aguilafuente, Madrona, Espirdo, Duratón and Castiltierra. This decline was further accentuated during the 200 years when the city and province were under Moorish domination.

With the Reconquest of Castile, the Castilian counts, with Fernán González at the head, repopulated the province with settlers from Galicia, Asturias, León, Vizcaya and La Rioja, who left their mark on many local toponyms. This was the period of the formation of the Community of the City and Lands of Segovia, with the construction of various beautiful Romanesque churches: Sotosalbos, Sepúlveda, Pedraza, Maderuelo, Fuentidueña, Sacramenia, etc.

Charles III coin.

The House of Trastámara, principally kings John II and Henry IV, brought a new era of splendour. An economic boom took place in the cloth industry, thanks to the excellent quality of the local Merino sheep, and Mudéjar workmen built such fine monuments as the Alcázar in Segovia, the castles of Coca and Cuéllar, parish churches, etc.

The War of the Communities, waged by Segovian nobles against the power of Charles I, saw the beginning of a new period of decadence in the province, though decline was once more halted by the royal undertakings of the new Bourbon dynasty in the 18th century, which included the construction of the Palace of the Granja de San Ildefonso and the creation in the Alcázar of Segovia of the Royal Artillery College.

The War of Independence also left its mark on the historical and economic development of the province. After the impulse of the Romantic period, 20th-century Segovia and its province can look to a future filled with hope and prosperity.

The abundance and diversity of the monumental sites in the province have made it a tourist destination of exceptional interest which, along with the local livestock farming, agriculture and related industry, form its principal source of

Painting representing Saint Francis of Borja and Charles V.

Detail of a capital in the Church of San Esteban.

income. On 4 December 1985, Segovia was declared **World Heritage** by UNESCO, in a declaration calling on its people to ensure the protection and conservation of its cultural and natural heritage.

The province of Segovia, covering an area of 6,947 km², is made up of two basic units of relief: the Sierra and the Meseta, which are linked by the Piedemonte, or piedmont. The altitude of the province ranges from the 750 metres of Remondo in the extreme northwest to a maximum of 2,430 metres in the Pico de Peñalara. It borders on the provinces of Burgos and Valladolid to the north, Soria to the east, Avila to the west and Madrid and Guadalajara to the south.

The local climate is continental, with harsh, often icy winters and short, hot summers. The drought which has often threatened the province is the origin of rogatory ceremonies known as **mojadas** held in the village of Caballar. According to legend, after burying Frutos in the hermitage in Duratón, his brother and sister Valentín and Engracia retired to Caballar, where they were martyrised by the Moors, who threw their heads into the Holy Fountain. Their bodies were buried beside that of Saint Frutos, but their heads remained in

Caballar, kept in a silver reliquary in the parish church. During periods of drought, they are carried in a procession to the Holy Fountain, where they are immersed in the water with a prayer for rain.

The festivities of the province have a markedly feminine character, as most of the local towns and villages celebrate with great pomp the Feast of Saint Agatha on 5 February, the Assumption of the Virgin on 15 August or the Nativity on 8 September. The popular dances and pilgrimages take place to the sound of the *tamboril,* a small drum, and the dolcian, an ancient instrument of Semite origin similar to the hornpipe. There now exists a school for dolcian players which has revived the instrument and popular music in the province, a work commenced in his day by the famous musicologist Agapito Marazuela.

Many are the dances and and tunes which liven up the festivities, but two are outstanding for their colour and

Celebrations of the Feast of Saint Anthony in Fuenterrebollo.

Arts and crafts: ceramics.

beauty of movement: the Castilian *jota* and the *paloteo.* The latter, a stick dance, is performed by Segovian lads with great skill and precision. The sticks even used to be replaced at times by ploughshares.

Another indispensable element in the festivities of Segovia are bulls, with famous *encierros* in Cuéllar, said to be the oldest in Spain, with traditional *corridas* in the Plaza Mayor, when a bullring is installed in the square as it was in medieval times.

If Segovian folklore is rich and varied, none less so is its gastronomy. Segovian *cuisine* is world-famous: some of its most outstanding dishes are **roast suckling** *(tostón),* **lamb, judiones** (beans) from **La Granja, trout, sopa castellana** (soup), **chorizo** (sausage) and **ham,** *candeal* **bread** cooked in a wood oven and, for dessert, **ponche segoviano** (biscuit made from egg-yolk and marzipan). These tasty dishes, excellently-prepared, are on the menu at restaurants throughout the capital and province.

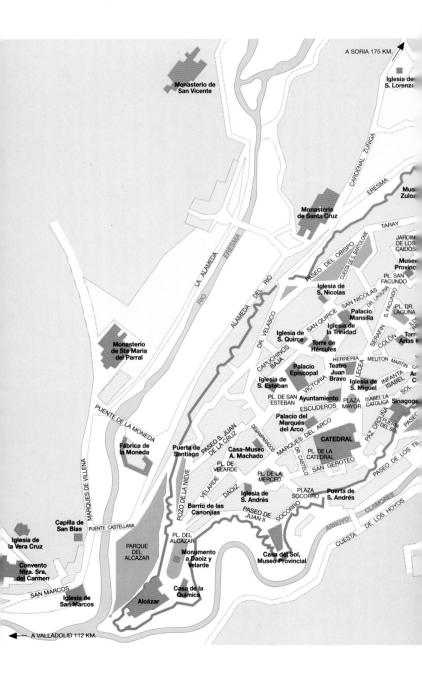

A SORIA 175 KM.

Iglesia de S. Lorenzo

Monasterio de San Vicente

CARDENAL ZUÑIGA

ERESMA

Mus
Zuloa

Monasterio de Santa Cruz

TARAY

JARDIN DE LOS CAIDOS

Museo Provinc

PASEO DEL OBISPO

CUESTA DE S. BARTOLOME

PL. SAN FACUNDO

LA. ALAMEDA.

ERESMA

ALAMEDA DEL RIO

Iglesia de S. Nicolas

DR. LAGUNA

SAN NICOLAS

PL. DR. LAGUNA

S. FACUNDO

RIO

DR. VELASCO

SAN QUIRCE

Palacio Mansilla

SERAFIN

COLÓN

Torr
Arias I

Monasterio de Sta Maria del Parral

Iglesia de S. Quirce

Iglesia de la Trinidad

Torre de Hércules

HERRERIA

LECEA

MELITON MARTIN

CAPUCHINOS BAJA

Palacio Episcopal

Teatro Juan Bravo

INFANTA ISABEL

Ar
C

Iglesia de S. Esteban

VICTORIA

Iglesia de S. Miguel

SOL

PUENTE DE LA MONEDA

PL. DE SAN ESTEBAN

Ayuntamiento

ESCUDEROS

PLAZA MAYOR

ISABEL LA CATOLICA

Sinagoga

PAZ ORDUÑA

PUER
DEL SOL

PASE

Palacio del Marqués del Arco

MARQUES DEL ARCO

Fábrica de la Moneda

Puerta de Santiago

PASEO S. JUAN DE LA CRUZ

DESAMPARADOS

CATEDRAL

PL. DE LA CATEDRAL

PASEO DE LOS TI

Casa-Museo A. Machado

MARQUES DE CASTELO

SAN GEROTEO

MARQUES DE VILLENA

PL. DE VELARDE

PL. DE LA MERCED

PLAZA SOCORRO

Puerta de S. Andrés

VELARDE

DAOIZ

Iglesia de S. Andrés

Capilla de San Blas

POZO DE LA NIEVE

PUENTE CASTELLANA

Barrio de las Canonjías

PASEO DE JUAN II

SOCORRO

ARROYO

CLAMORES

DE LOS HOYOS

Iglesia de la Vera Cruz

PL. DEL ALCAZAR

CUESTA

Convento Ntra. Sra. del Carmen

PARQUE DEL ALCAZAR

Monumento a Daoiz y Velarde

Casa del Sol, Museo Provincial

SAN MARCOS

Iglesia de San Marcos

Casa de la Química

Alcázar

A VALLADOLID 112 KM.

8

ANTONIO CORONEL

POZO

CARRETERA DE BOCEGUILLAS

AV. DEL PADRE CLARET

A LA GRANJA 11 KM.

PL. DEL
SALVADOR

Acueducto Romano

PL. DEL
SALVADOR

Convento de
San Antonio
El Real

LARGA

OCHOA
ONDATEGUI

S. ALFONSO RODRÍGUEZ

FERNÁN GARCÍA ALMIRA

LAS. Mª RENÁS

SANTA ISABEL

Iglesia
Santa Isabel

CAMPILLO

DE
ARES

Casa del
Marques
Lozoya

cio
nde
ste

PL. DEL
CONDE
CHESTE

Casa de las
Cadenas

Palacio
Quintanar

Iglesia
San Justo

Iglesia
San Salvador

SAN ANTÓN

SAN

BARRIHUELO

PL. CAÑO
GRANDE

A MADRID
(Guadarrama)
70 KM.

ENCIADO
PERALTA

Iglesia S.
Sebastián

SAN JUAN

PL. DE LA
ARTILLERIA

PLAZA DE
DIAZ SANZ

ALFEREZ
PROVISIONAL

PLAZA DEL
ALTO DE
LOS LEONES

A MADRID
(Navacerrada)
91 KM.
A AVILA 70 KM.

CONDE DE
GAZZOLA

PL. DEL
AZOGUEJO

SAN FRANCISCO

Academia
de Artillería

BUITRAGO

Y VIDA

PLATA

JOSE ZORRILLA

Seminario

GRABADOR ESPINOSA

CERVANTES

MUERTE

INDEPENDENCIA

HILANDERAS

ROBLE

JARDIN BOTANICO

E LOS
EJOS

Casa de
los Río

Casa
de los
Picos

Mirador
de la
Canaleja

Casa
de la
Tierra

AV. FERNÁNDEZ LADREDA

Casa del
Sello de
Paños

Iglesia
S. Clemente

GOBERNADOR

FDEZ. JIMENEZ

JARDIN
BOTANICO

MORILLA

SARTEN

AN
JUAN BRAVO

Palacio
del Conde
de Alpuente

CARMEN

Casa de
Ayala
Berganza

SANTO TOMÁS

n

Alhóndiga

PL. DEL
DR. GILA

CARRETAS

Iglesia
San Millán

PASEO DEL CONDE DE SEPÚLVEDA

TE. SANTI-SPIRITU

SAN MILLÁN

CABALLEROS

SANTO

DOMINGO

DE SILOS

PASEO DE EZEQUIEL GONZALEZ

BARREROS

ANTIGUA CTRA. DE MADRONA

DE LA PIEDAD

SAN

VELODROMO

ROQUE

CAMINO

CARRETERA N-110

Night-time view of the Cathedral.

ITINERARY 1

The first itinerary is devoted to the capital. To get to know the capital in just one day we will have to get up early and organise our tour around three outstanding monuments: **the Aqueduct, the Cathedral and the Alcázar.** After lunch in any of the local *mesones* or restaurants, we can continue our visit in the outskirts, pausing in Vera Cruz, Fuencisla and El Parral districts.

SEGOVIA CAPITAL

The city of Segovia stands on an elongated rock running from east to west at approximately 1,000 metres above sea level. It is surrounded by two rivers, the Eresma to the north and the Clamores to the south. These converge towards the west, at the foot of the Alcázar.

Panoramic view of the city.

The Cathedral.

The great mystery of the Romanisation of the city is the construction of the Aqueduct, one of the most imposing monuments in the entire Roman world, in a city whose name is scarcely mentioned in the annals of ancient history, and which only preserves a few rustic funeral stones from Roman times. During Visigoth times, it was episcopal see, and this culture left its traces in the necropolis just outside the city. In 1088, Count Raymond of Burgundy repopulated the city, which saw the construction of churches, palaces and small bourgeois houses. Romanesque art flourished, in Segovia characterised by porches of arcades supported by paired columns, encircling the local churches on one, two or three sides. The poor structure of fabrics, often covered with wood, was compensated for by the ornamental richness of cornices and capitals.

During the 14th and 15th centuries, the city rose to eminence thanks to the House of Trastámara, and many Mudéjar monuments were built. From the 16th century on, Segovia began an economic and cultural decline until the fire of the Alcázar in 1862 caused a revival in construction which, in the 20th century, is reflected in the urbanisation of promenades and the creation of industrial estates.

Detail of the Roman Aqueduct.

Aerial view of Segovia with the Aqueduct spanning the city.

The city of Segovia, meeting-point of various cultures, offers a monumental site around which our visit should revolve: the Aqueduct, the Cathedral and the Alcázar.

The Aqueduct, the Cathedral and the Alcázar.

The **Aqueduct** is one of the most staggering works of the Roman period. Built to bring water from the River Acebeda to the upper districts of the city, it starts close to the La Granja road with small arches which gradually increase in height to the double arches in Plaza del Azoguejo, where they measure 29 metres in height. The Aqueduct is 728 metres long and contains a total of 167 arches. It was built in the early-2nd century using granite blocks with no mortar to join them.

The late-Gothic **Cathedral** began to be built in 1525. Its elegance and grace have won it the nickname of «The Lady of Cathedrals». Inside are treasures impossible to enumerate. From the former Cathedral of Santa María which stood in the Alcázar gardens, the beautiful cloister by Juan Guas and the choirstalls, both dating back to the 15th century, were transferred to the new building. Of the eighteen chapels in the Cathedral, one of the most outstanding is that of El Santo Entierro or La Piedad, which features a triptych of the «Descent from the Cross» by Ambrosio Benson (early-16th century), and the Altarpiece of La Piedad by Juan de Juni, carved in 1571. The Chapel of Los Santos Cosme y Damián contains an «Immaculate» by Gregorio Fernández, whilst the Chapel of El Cristo Yacente has a sculpture of Christ recumbent by the same artist. The Chapel of El Sacramento, with classical portal, houses sculptor Manuel Pereira's «Christ of the Agony», framed by a ceramic altarpiece made in 1895 by Daniel Zuloaga. The choirstalls, the neoclassical altarpiece of the retrochoir, the stained-glass windows and the high vaults complete the harmonious vision of Segovia Cathedral.

Plaza Mayor and the Cathedral, Segovia.

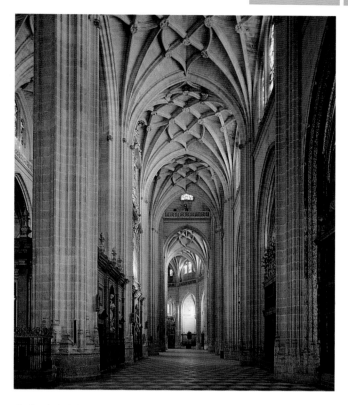

Cathedral cloister.

«Pieta» by Juan de Juni.

The Alcázar, seen from La Fuencisla.

The **Alcázar** is the civil building which best symbolises the city of Segovia. Originally built as a fortress, its origins are uncertain, but there is no doubt that it is Roman or earlier. Under the kings of the House of Trastámara, it was converted into an Oriental-style palace. Charles III installed the Artillery College in it, but in 1862 it suffered a fire which destroyed much of the buildings. After restoration work was completed in 1980, the General Military Archives were installed in the Alcázar.

The Sala del Solio, the Sala de la Galera, that of Las Piñas and the Salón de Reyes are rooms all adorned with magnificent ceilings and Morisco plasterwork, most of them restored. The apartments are all fitted with period furniture, armour and paintings. The Juan II Tower commands magnificent views once one has toiled up its 156 steep steps.

Chamber of the Kings.

The King's Bedroom, adorned with beautiful painted sargas.

*Church of
San Andrés.*

*Church of
San Millán.*

Church of San Martín and the monument to Juan Bravo.

Romanesque churches

Of the 30 Romanesque churches Segovia boasted in its period of maximum splendour, 18 remain, eleven of them still used for worship and the others converted to other uses. For the most part, they stand in the square bearing the same name as the respective church, and include the following:

San Millán, in the old Moorish quarter, has a strong resemblance to Jaca. It dates to the first half of the 12th century. The exterior is adorned with a square dome, Mudéjar tower and two lovely arcaded courtyards. The interior feature the magnificent vault of the dome, carvings by Segovian sculptor Aniceto Marinas and mural paintings.

San Martín is situated in one of the finest squares in Segovia, Plaza de las Sirenas. Its original structure is pre-Romanesque, with ground plan in the shape of a Greek cross to which were added three apses and three porticoes. The church takes on exceptional interest thanks to the carving of its capitals, along with works by Gregorio Fernández and Pedro de Mena and Flemish paintings in the interior.

La Trinidad was built in the 12th century over the remains of an earlier church, probably Mozarabic. This is one of the best-preserved churches in Segovia. The interior features a painting of «The Holy Face» by Ambrosio Benson and a fine Gothic chapel.

La Vera Cruz stands in the San Marcos district adjoining the Zamarramala road. It was built in 1208 by the Knights Templar. The ground plan is a 12-sided polygon with an earlier tower adjoining the church.

San Lorenzo, in the district of the same name, is one of the best examples of Romanesque brick construction, unusual in Segovia. Inside, the Plateresque Chapel of San Marcos is the most interesting feature.

Of the original building, the **Church of San Esteban** conserves only the tower and the atrium. The tower was burnt down in 1896 in a fire caused by lightning, restoration work being completed in 1928. Inside is a fine 13th-century «Calvary».

Church of San Esteban.

Church of La Vera Cruz.

Other Romanesque buildings, though restored, include the churches of **San Andrés, San Sebastián, San Clemente,** with excellent mural paintings on the theme of the Tree of Jesse; **Santo Tomás, San Marcos, el Salvador** and **San Justo,** also with interesting mural paintings. This list completes our summary of the most interesting Romanesque churches in Segovia.

Other religious buildings

Interesting **churches from other periods** include: **San Miguel,** built after the original building, in whose atrium Isabel the Catholic was crowned, was destroyed in 1532; the **Church of El Seminario,** built in Herreran style in the late-16th century; the **Church of El Corpus Christi,** 13th-century former Jewish synagogue, where the Miracle of the Sacred Form took place in 1410: and the **Sanctuary of La Fuencisla,** which dates back to the 16th century. The different districts and winding streets of Segovia are also dotted with many convents and monasteries: the **Monastery of El Parral,** in La

Alameda, was founded by Henry IV in 1445 and patronised by the Marquis of Villena. It is the work of Juan Guas, and is Gothic in style. The Plateresque tower is by Juan Campero (16th century) and the high altarpiece dates back to the same period. The monastery is inhabited by monks of the Hieronymite order.

The **Convent of Santa Cruz la Real** was founded in the 13th century by Saint Dominic. The Catholic Monarchs ordered the construction of the present building, which features a lovely portal and Gothic spires, in the 15th century. The garden within has a cave where Saint Dominic did penance.

San Antonio el Real was built as a pleasure palace for Henry IV in the site known as «El Campillo». The high chapel has a magnificent Morisco ceiling and a fine Flemish altarpiece. The convent is occupied by enclosed Franciscan nuns.

The **Convent of Carmelitas Descalzas** in La Alameda de la Fuencisla, was founded by John of the Cross in 1588. Inside is the tomb of the saint and a small Carmelite museum.

The **Monastery of San Vicente el Real** is the oldest in the city. In the year 140 there was a temple to Jupiter, which was destroyed by fire, on this site. Inside the monastery are interesting tombs of abbesses.

Panoramic view of the Monastery of El Parral.

Convent of Santa Cruz la Real.

Civil buildings

Besides its religious buildings, Segovia also boasts many magnificent civil constructions, such as the city walls, and a good number of palaces and turretted houses going back to various periods. Of the original seven city gates, only three still stand, San Cebrián, Santiago and San Andrés, as well as three posterns. Amongst the city's towers are those of Hercules (12th century) in the Convent of Las Dominicanas; the **Torreón de Lozoya** (14th) in Plaza de San Martín; and that of Arias Dávila (15th) in Plaza de los Huertos.

In Plaza del Conde de Cheste are a number of 15th-century palaces conferring a special charm on the square: the **Palace of Quinanar,** the **House of Segovia** or of Las Cadenas, the **House of Lozoya** and the **Palace of the Count of Cheste.** Calle Real, for its part, contains the Casa de los Picos, the **Palace of the Count of Alpuente,** now the Delegation of Public Works, and the **Casa de la Alhóndiga.** The walls of almost all the palaces are covered with the typical patterns or engravings. The **Palace of the Marquis of Arco** and the **Episcopal Palace** both date to the 16th century.

The city also has various museums and private collections open to the public. These include the **Provincial Fine Arts Museum,** the **Zuloga Museum,** the **Cathedral Museum** and the Antonio Machado House-**Museum.**

Portrait of Antonio Machado.

Lozoya Tower.

Other aspects of Segovia

The busiest spot in the city is Plaza Mayor with the Town Hall, its arcades and the Teatro Juan Bravo. The terraces and surrounding streets are full of cafés and mesones serving typical dishes and offering the visitor the chance to rest after the visit to the city.

Segovia celebrates its holidays with great enthusiasm: the emotive processions of Holy Week; the Saint John's Day and Saint Peter's Day celebrations from 24 to 30 June; the catorcena, in penance to the Holy of Holies, on the first Sunday in September; and, the last Sunday of the month, the *romería* (religious procession) of La Fuencisla. These holidays feature performances of jotas and other popular dances, to the sound of the *tamboril* and the dolcian, the dancers wearing traditional costume.

The arts and crafts of Segovia feature particularly needlework made from *Segovian point,* ceramics, basketwork and souvenirs in general. Good shopping areas are to be found in Calle Real, Calle del Marqués de Arco and the market held every Thursday in Plaza de los Huertos.

Front of the Palace of Riofrío.

ITINERARY 2

Itinerary 2, 50 kilometres in all, takes in the zone of the Reales Sitios, revealing, in the midst of spectacular scenery, the palaces of La Granja and Riofrío. After having lunch in La Granja or vicinity we can enjoy a visit to the Real Sitio and the beauty of its gardens and fountains.

RIOFRIO

Surrounding by leafy oak woods some ten kilometres from Segovia is the *Royal Site* of Riofrío. In the early-18th century, the forest of Riofrío belonged to a Segovian noble, the Marquis of Paredes, a descendant of Juan Bravo. The hunting grounds contained many head of big game, something which made Philip V determined to acquire it. In 1724, the king obtained a lease on the site, which in 1751 became a royal possession through a contract of purchase and sale. After the death of Philip, his widow, Isabel of Farnesio, decided to convert this small manor into a *royal site* on the lines of El Pardo or the neighbouring San Ildefonso.

The sumptuous building was designed by the Italian architect Virgilio Rabaglio, assistant to Juvara in Turin and in the construction of the Palacio Real in Madrid. On the death of Rabaglio, the work was taken over by Carlos Frasquina and José Díaz Gamones. In 1579, Ferdinand VI died and Isabel of Farnesio became queen regent, losing her interest in the Riofrío work. Of her vast plan, only the palace was finally built, along with part of the Casa de Oficios and other dependencies. What has given Riofrío such a sentimental importance is the fact that the king consort, Francis of Assisi, husband of Isabel II, passed long periods here. It was also the place chosen by Alphonse XII to mourn the death of Queen Mercedes in 1878. The palace has a perfect square ground plan, each side measuring 84 metres. It is made from granite (the jambs and

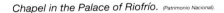

Chapel in the Palace of Riofrío. (Patrimonio Nacional).

Salón de Honor in the Hunting Museum. (Patrimonio Nacional).

windows) and masonry, plastered and painted pink which, contrasting with the pale apple green of the carpentry work, gives the palace a peculiar charm.

The three architectural elements most worthy of attention are the **patio,** the **chapel** and the **staircase,** as well as the rooms forming the different apartments. The paintings, tapestries and furniture were all chosen with the most exquisite taste to decorate this palace which, despite its size, was used as a hunting pavilion. Of particular interest are the 149 paintings depicting the «Life of Jesus Christ» in the first two rooms, the works by Lucas Jordán, the Alphonse XII bedroom (conserved just as it was when the monarch came here in mourning for Queen Mercedes) and the apartments of King Francis, with furniture and paintings of the highest quality, as the consort was a great art-lover and collector.

VALSAIN

Alphonso XI's book on the art of hunting defined Valsaín as a **royal mountain of bear and boar.** This is a very true observation, as it was the wealth of game in these woods which attracted the kings of Castile, great hunters all, to the area. In 1552, Philip II, whilst still a prince, ordered his architect, Gaspar de Vega, to build a palace here on the site where the hunting lodge known as the **Casa del Bosque** had stood since the times of Henry III.

The Palace of Valsaín was the birthplace of Princess Isabel Clara Eugenia in 1556, and suffered a fire in 1697 during the reign of Charles II. The Forest of Valsaín is one of the most magnificent natural beauty-spots in the provinces, and ICONA has equipped such sites as the **Boca del Asno** and **Los Asientos** to allow visitors an unforgettable day in the country. Also highly recommended is the September festivities, held in honour of the Virgin of the Rosary.

Scenery in La Boca de Asno.

Main front of the Palacio Real.

LA GRANJA DE SAN ILDEFONSO

The *Royal Site* of La Granja de San Ildefonso is 11 kilometres from Segovia and 77 from Madrid. The town lies on the north side of the Sierra de Guadarrama at an altitude of 1,191 metres, enjoying a pleasant, healthy climate. The site already existed in times of Henry III, who used it as a hunting lodge. Henry IV had it enlarged, and the Catholic Monarchs donated it to the monks of El Parral for their use and administration. Philip converted the old hunting pavilion into a palace after the style of the Alcázar in Madrid, El Pardo and El Escorial.

When Philip V and Isabel of Farnesio visited the place, they decided to use it as a retreat from time to time. To this end, they signed a contract for the acquisition of the site with the monks of El Parral and commissioned Teodoro Ardemans with the construction of the palace. Work began on 1 April 1721,

directed by assistant architect Juan Roman. The palace is a large, rectangular building with two parallel wings forming two inner courtyards, the Patio De Coches and the Patio De la Herradura. The central space occupied by the Patio of La Fuente, former cloister of the Hieronymite monastery, in Herreran severity. The masonry walls of the palace are plastered with architraved spaces filled with granite, and slate-roofed turrets. The main front, overlooking the gardens, was designed by Juvara in 1734 and completed by Juan Bautista Sachetti. The interior of the palace is divided into two floors. The ceilings in the ground floor rooms are painted with mythological scenes, the work of Bartolomé Rusca. The **Sala de la Fuente** («Fountain Room») is thus known due to the fountain installed in the centre of the wall, adorned with a bust of Christine of Sweden. On either side are busts in Carrara marble symbolising Day and Night. The **Marble Room** is adorned by marbles from all over Spain, including the busts of Louis I, son of Philip I, and his wife. The next rooms feature such interesting works as paintings on glass by Lucas Jordán, the «Adoration of the Magi» and «Adoration of the Shepherds»; paintings symbolising the five senses from the Isabel of Farnesio collection; and the monumental sculpture of «Veiled Faith» by Frémin.

The office, situated on the first floor of the Palacio Real. (Patrimonio Nacional).

The Throne Room. (Patrimonio Nacional).

The frescoes adorning the first-floor rooms were destroyed by fire in 1918. The dining-room is interesting, featuring various still life paintings. The **office** has the altarpiece of «The Family of Philip V» by Lozano Valle, a copy of the original by Van Loo; the **portrait** of «Charles III» by Molinareto; and the cabinet-desk of Francis of Assisi. The **throne room** features a fine silver-embroidered canopy dating to the times of Charles IV. The former **antechamber** of the founding monarchs contains a fine 18th-century Portuguese bed. From here, we go to the **Tapestry Museum,** which occupies rooms on the ground and first floors, organised to this end after the fire. The works exhibited date to the 16th, 17th and 18th centuries, with important series such as the «History of Ciro», «The Honours» and others made in Brussels workshops.

The palace is completed by the **collegiate church,** situated in the west front. Its ground plan is in the shape of a Latin cross, with a high dome and two towers. The founding monarchs are buried here.

Around the palace are distributed the remaining dependencies, such as the canons' house, the Casa de Oficios, the bodyguards' barracks and the stables. In 1918, a terrible fire destroyed much of these annex buildings, as well as some of the rooms in the palace.

The buildings are surrounded by beautiful, extensive gardens, lakes and a large park. The design of the garden and the statues which adorn it was carried out by a French team including Boutelou and Carlier. Philip V had the lime trees brought here from Holland, chestnuts from the Indies, and other species to form the great wood. Renato Frémin and Juan Thierry carved the statues, urns and groups of lead cast and painted white to imitate Carrara marbles from 1721 onwards. Opposite the main front is the scenography of the **«Great Cascade»** or **«New Cascade».** To the right of this pool is the **Fountain of the Four Winds,** featuring the god Aeolus, ruler of the winds, and the four enchained Zephyrs.

At the top of the waterfall is the **Fountain of the Three Graces,** by Frémin, and behind it is a kiosk in pink stone from Sepúlveda, in the French style of Louis XIV. Other interesting fountains are those of **«The Forest»**, **«Pomona»** and, above all, the large, terraced group at the rear, **«The Horse-Race»,** made up of three ponds and various fountains.

Creation Room. Tapestry Museum. (Patrimonio Nacional).

Collegiate Church.

From here, those interested in taking a walk can admire the artificial lake known as **«The Sea»,** whose waters reflect the sombre cone of the rock known as **Silla del Rey** («King's Stone»). Those not feeling up to the climb to the sea can return towards the palace, passing through **Plaza de las Ocho Calles.** Here is a central group representing Mercury carrying Psyche, who holds the pome of beauty, in his arms. Around this group are eight fountains, all of them formed by a pond with a semicircular arch supported by Ionic columns and containing the corresponding deity: Saturn, Minerva, Hercules, Ceres, Neptune, Victory, Mars or Sybil.

One of the tree-lined paths leading from the square towards the square pond leads to the **Fountain of El Canastillo,** whose play of water, made up of 32 oblique spouts, is perhaps the most impressive of all.

The **Fountain of Latona,** or **Fountain of the Frogs,** has a beautiful play of water with the sculptural groups of the Scythian clowns turned into frogs by Latona after they refused to let her children, Apollo and Diana, drink water.

From this fountain we come to the «**Baths of Diana**», architecturally the most important fountain in the gardens. It was the last to be built, and was completed in 1742 according to plans drawn up by Santiago Bousseau.

The beauty of the flowerbeds and the numerous fine statues and urns adorning the **Garden of Fame** make this the master-piece of the San Ildefonso gardens.

Besides the palace, other important monuments in the town include the **Parish Church of Nuestra Señora del Rosario,** built in 1752, containing the «Santísimo Cristo del Perdón».

The **Chapel of Nuestra Señora de los Dolores** was built in 1743.

Another interesting building is the Glass and Crystal Factory, one of the few remaining examples of 18th-century industrial architecture.

Fountain of the Baths of Diana.

Dusk over the Romanesque Church of Sotosalbos.

ITINERARY 3

Itinerary 3 offers us a splendid sample of Segovian Romanesque, ranging from feudal manors to religious buildings. The repopulation of the province during the 11th century explains the existence of these veritable jewels of Romanesque art, even in such surprising localities as the Duratón Gorge. The route is a total of 160 km long, approximately.

SOTOSALBOS

Sotosalbos lies on the northern flanks of the cordillera, 18 km from the capital between Somosierra and Guadarrama, below the Malagosto mountain pass.

The most historic Segovian documents mention Sotosalbos as early as 1122, when Alphonse I of Aragon, husband of Queen Urraca of Castile, donated to the Cathedral and the bishop of Segovia an inheritance in the district of **Sotis Albis.** In the 13th century, in 1220 to be precise, the township was consolidated by receiving the **Carta Puebla,** that is its own municipal charter, setting the taxes to be paid to the lord by the inhabitants.

The principal monumental attraction of Sotosalbos is its Romanesque church, built in the 11th century though with later additions such as the 12th-century portico and tower and other features dating to the 14th century. The gallery is of almost undescribable beauty, centring on a portal with zig-zagging adornment and flanked by four semicircular arches and three slightly oval arches. The capitals and cornices of this gallery features a magnificent sculpture of medieval themes such as the fight between Roland and Ferragut, two mythical characters.

Inside, the church has a single nave, with a square-shaped apse from the original building, the walls adorned with re-cently-discovered Romanesque frescoes. The tower can be reached from the interior through a simple Romanesque portal. Amongst the most precious items in the museum are the statues of the Virgin of the Sierra, patron saint; the 14th-century Gothic «Christ of Health»; the processional cross by Segovian silversmith Oquendo; and the Gothic panels attributed to Nicolás Francés or the Master of the Carnations, all of which is worthy of our attention, as is the Romanesque baptismal font.

Another of the attractions of Sotosalbos are the numerous

Detail of the Romanesque Church of Sotosalbos.

festivities celebrated throughout the year: **Saint Agatha** on 5 February or the nearest Sunday, when the locals where typical costume, dances are held and *chorizo* (a kind of salami), wine and local buns, or *bollos,* are offered; the Feast of the **Virgin of the Sierra,** held on the Saturday, Sunday and Monday of Pentecost; the traditional *romería* of mountaineers to the **Malagosto pass,** and other minor fiestas such as those of Saint Anthony of Padua, Mary Magdalene, Saint Isidoro and Saint Michael.

PEDRAZA

The town of Pedraza, 37 km from Segovia, lies at the foot of the Sierra de Guadarrama on a rocky hillock flanked by the Batanes and San Miguel streams, tributaries of the River Cega.
The prosperity of the Community of Pedraza during medieval times lay in its flocks of Merino sheep, whose wool was woven in the looms of Segovia or exported to Bruges or Florence. This allowed the local sheep farmers to become rich, settling in the town to enjoy the right this gave of pasturing their flocks in the fields of the Community.
Of the many churches Pedraza once boasted, Santa María, Santo Domingo, San Martín, San Sebastián, San Pedro and

Church of Nuestra Señora de las Vegas.

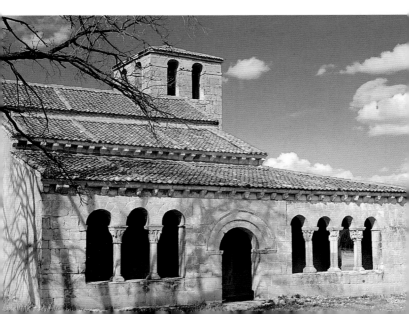

Gate of Pedraza Castle.

San Juan, only this last still remains more or less intact and open to the public. It stands in Plaza Mayor, and features a Romanesque tower with high windows. The lower part of the town also has two interesting hermitages: that of **Nuestra Señora del Carrascal,** with a Romanesque portal, and that of **La Florida,** with rustic Romanesque apse, now converted into a private home.

Pedraza has always been a well-guarded walled city, and its only access, the Puerta de la Cárcel, or Prison Gate, was closed at nightfall until recently. This gate and sole access to Pedraza forms part of the wall adjoining the former prison. Over its arches is the escutcheon of the city condestable, the former head of the local militia.

The way along Calle Real to Plaza Mayor is dotted with such noble houses and palaces as that of the Castros, the Zamarriegos, the so-called **House of Pilate,** that of the Marquises of La Floresta, that of the Bernaldo de Quirós, etc. This stroll prepares us for the enormous surprise awaiting us in **Plaza Mayor,** a wide square with arcades, old houses and the city hall with its open arches and clocktower. Adjoining the Church of San Juan is the peculiar **green balcony,** ordered built by Juan Pérez de la Torre so as to get a better view of the

Pedraza Castle.

bullfights in the square, and the palaces of the Marquises of Lozoya and that of the Mirandas, which houses the magnificent Taberna del Alcalde, a sight not to be missed.

From Plaza Mayor we enter Plaza del Ganado, where cattle-dealers met during the local fairs. The most characteristic aspect of this square is its monumental, hundred-year-old elm tree. From here we come to the castle esplanade, where we can see the ruins of the Church of Santa María.

Pedraza Castle stands on a privileged position: to one side is the side of a steep ravine, whilst on the other it overlooks the esplanade separating it from the houses of the town, divided from it by the moat and a high, strong barbican with round turrets. It was built in 1516 by the Condestable of Castile, Pedro Fernández de Velasco, whose coat of arms features over the castle gate, made of black poplar covered by iron spikes and flanked by two large sentry boxes. The festivities of Pedraza take place from 8 to 12 September in honour of the patron saint of the town, the Virgin of El Carrascal, and feature a solemn procession and bullfighting in Plaza Mayor. The *caldereta* and *jotas* combine to create a spectacle full of colour and tradition.

CASTILNOVO

Eight km from Sepúlveda, between juniper and oak woods, rises the unmistakable silhouette of the **castle,** the best-conserved of all Segovian fortresses. A legendary tale has it that it was built by the Moorish king of Sepúlveda in around the year 775, though it is, in fact, a Mudéjar work dating to around 1300. With a square ground plan, the castle is adorned with bands and friezes in red brick, typical of the Mudéjar style. On its north side are two powerful semicircular towers whilst a third, in the centre, has a curious spiral staircase.

The building is reasonably well-preserved, in spite of the transformations it has undergone at the hands of its various occupants. In the 15th century, it belonged to Alvaro de Luna, who left us his escutcheons. After his dramatic beheading in the Plaza Mayor of Valladolid, the castle passed into the hands of the Velasco family, whilst in the 19th century Queen Isabel II gave it to the Catalan painter José Galofre, its principal restorer, and since 1983 it has been owned by Castilnovo, SA.

Castilnovo Castle.

SEPULVEDA

The town of Sepúlveda lies on uneven ground over hills, ridges and gullies, over the canyons of the Duratón and Castilla rivers, 59 km from Segovia. Dominating the surrounding houses stands, on an isolated ridge, the Church of El Salvador and, at the other end, more solitary, that of Nuestra Señora de la Peña.

Inhabited since time immemorial, it was the *Septem Publica* of Roman times, a name thought by some to refer to the seven doors it possessed during the Middle Ages. Only four now remain: the Arch of La Villa, that of Ecce Homo or El Azogue, the Gate of La Fuerza and the Gate of El Río.

Alphonse I first captured the town from the Moors in 746, and it was later, repopulated by Fernán González. Finally reconquered in 1010 by Sancho García, it was populated and rebuilt under the reign of Alphonse VI.

Sepúlveda was capital of a Community of Town and Lands, and gave its name to the charter known as the **Fuero de Sepúlveda.**

Outstanding among its historic monuments are the medieval churches dating to the time of repopulation. **El Salvador,**

Overall view of Sepúlveda with, in the background, the Church of El Salvador.

A street in Sepúlveda.

perched on a hill in the centre of the town, is a Romanesque church built in the 11th century, the first in the entire province. **Santa María de la Peña** is a Romanesque sanctuary dedicated to the patron saint of the Community of the Town and Lands. At its head is a powerful three-storey tower with a square ground plan with an inscription stating the name of its author, **Dominicus Iuliani,** and the date of its construction, 1144.

San Bartolomé, close to the central square, has a beautiful access with staircase, and a stone crossing, though its apse and tower are simple examples of Romanesque art.

The **Church of San Justo,** situated just past the town arch, is an originally Romanesque building with Renaissance additions, whilst the ruins of the **Church of Santiago** conserve a strong tower made from masonry and with the air of a defensive structure, rare in this region.

The strategic position and historic importance of Sepúlveda

Church of El Salvador (Sepúlveda).

led to the construction of its strong, broad walls. Besides the four entrance gates, also still standing is the **castle,** inside the walls of which stands a later baroque mansion.

Like all Castilian towns worthy of the name, Sepúlveda's **Plaza Mayor** is the most important, liveliest spot. It is presided over by the former **Town Hall,** built in the 17th century. The **Town Arch,** adjoining Plaza Mayor, leads into Plaza San Justo where, opposite the church of the same name, is the emblazoned mansion of the González Sepúlveda family, known popularly as the Casa del Moro. Sepúlveda holds its local feast in honour of its patron saint, the Virgin of the Rock, in late-August. Also worth seeing are the Holy Week processions and the festivities for Saint James the Apostle on 25 July, with bullfighting in the tiny Plaza Mayor.

Local arts and crafts include articles made from the popular pink stone from the nearby quarries, and leatherwork.

SAN FRUTOS DE DURATON

This former monks' priory stands amidst splendid scenery to the north of Sepúlveda. After the village of Villaseca, a track leads us along the five km to the **Gorges of the River Duratón.**

This difficult path commands spectacular, unforgettable views over Castile.

At a bend in the river, over a kind of tiny peninsula, stands the church and part of what was once the famous Priory of San Frutos. The fabric of the church is Romanesque, dating to the 11th century. In 1076, Alphonse VI donated this site to the Monastery of Silos, and a few years later master architect Michel, at the orders of Fortunio, Abbot of Silos, constructed the church in early Castilian Romanesque style. The present apse and the gallery on the south side were built in the 12th century.

It was here in around the year 680 that Saint Frutos did penance with his brother and sister, Valentin and Engracia. Legend has it that Frutos faced the Moorish hosts, drawing a line in the earth with his staff over which the enemy could not pass. For this reason, the steep rock is known as the **Cuchillada de San Frutos** («The Slash of Saint Frutos»).

On 25 October, feast day of the holy hermitage, a *romería,* or religious procession takes place, gathering together people from all over the province to venerate Saint Frutos.

Gorges of the River Duratón.

ITINERARY 4

Itinerary 4 takes us to magnificent towns defended by strong castles, and agricultural lands with thick pinewoods («pinares» in Spanish), for which reason it is known as the Tierra de Pinares. These are locations of great historical importance where many civilisations have left their mark: the Vacceos, Arevacos, Romans, Visigoths and Moors, the latter causing the area to be graced with works in the later Mudéjar style. The total distance of this itinerary is around 150 km.

SANTA MARIA LA REAL DE NIEVA

This town stands on a slatestone hill, dominating the cereal-growing plains some 31 km from Segovia. It was founded by Catherine of Lancaster, wife of Henry III, after the miraculous apparition of the Virgin, a statue of whom was found in an underground site by a shepherd from nearby Nieva in 1392. Around the sanctuary was erected a large building, occupied by Dominican monks between 1414 and 1432. The monastery is a surprising, beautiful architectural monument whose outstanding element is its soaring tower, in two sections.

Church of Nuestra Señora de Soterraña.

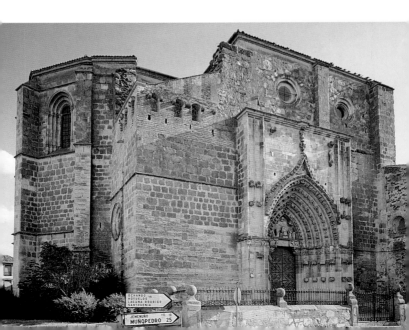

Detail of a capital in the Church of Nuestra Señora de Soterraña.

Though no longer as flourishing as it was during the 15th and 16th centuries, the town still bears many witnesses to its glorious history: ancient mansions, with various different escutcheons around the **Media Luna,** the street to the rear of the Town Hall, and an old café, dating to the early-20th century, where people from the town and surrounding countryside gather to while away the time.

The **Church of Nuestra Señora de la Soterraña** is a broad Gothic building with a nave and two aisles and high vaults. The choir has an impressive baroque organ, with another in the wall on the side of the epistle, and a long gilt altar dating to the 17th century and dedicated to Dominican saints. The cloister is a remarkable work of Castilian medieval art, built in the full Gothic period though in an archaic transitional style. Its conception was perhaps a caprice of Catherine of Lancaster, as it is reminiscent of late English Gothic-Romanesque art.

In September, the streets and main square here are filled with life in celebration of the Feast of the Virgin of Soterraña, which begins on 7 September with the **offering of the candles** in the four main streets, each bearing the name of the villages to which they lead: Nieva, Ochanda, Ortigosa and Pascuales.

Continuing along our route, we come to nearby **Nieva,** where we can admire the Romanesque brick church (13th century) devoted to Saint Stephen, the protomartyr.

Cloister of the Monastery of Santa María la Real de Nieva.

NAVA DE LA ASUNCION

This is one of the most flourishing towns in the province. It is surrounded by pinewoods, and its industry dynamism is based on the exploitation of its extraordinary wealth in wood, as well as on ceramics and flour-making factories.

The Parish Church of Nuestra Señora de la Asunción, a baroque brick building, is spacious, giving us an indication of the importance of the town in times gone by. But perhaps the most characteristic monument in the town is the **Caño del Obispo,** a neoclassical fountain erected by Fray Sebastián, Bishop of Osma. The area around it was recently urbanised, and a colossal bronze figure dedicated to «el fraile», as Sebastián is affectionately known to the local people, by Segovian sculptor José María García Moro, was installed.

The celebrations in honour of the Holy Christ of the Expiation take place the week after 14 September each year, with procession, spectacular night-time encierros and bullfights. These events attract crowds of people to the town from all over the province.

COCA

The houses of this town stand on the edge of a meseta, where the black and Italian poplar trees of the plain contrast with the bright green of the pines and the yellow stains of the cereal fields. Three silhouettes stand out from afar: the high Romanesque tower of the Church of San Nicolás, the profile of the church, and the castle. Few towns have a richer history. It was the **Cauca Vaccea,** which gave Rome nothing less than an emperor, Theodosius I, in the 4th century. During the Middle Ages it was the feud of the powerful Fonseca family of Portugal; Alonso de Fonseca, magnate at the court of Henry IV and bishop of Seville, ordered the splendid fortress built in the early-15th century.

Witnesses to its medieval past as head of a council are the Mudéjar gate known as the **Arco de la Vila** and the tower in the same style, pertaining to the **Church of San Nicolás,** now no longer standing.

But the most interesting building, along with the castle, is the **Church of Santa María la Mayor,** a spacious building dating to the late-Gothic period. The church has a fine Plateresque altarpiece and features the statues and tombs of its founders, the Fonseca family.

Fonseca family sepulchre in the Church of Santa María la Mayor.

Gothic-Mudéjar Castle, Coca.

The **castle,** built of brick throughout, is one of the most beautiful in the Peninsula, a masterpiece of Morisco stonemasons, fine workers in brick. The castle presently houses the National School of Forestry Management.

The local holidays take place on 3 May, day of the Exaltation of the Cross, and from 15 to 18 August in honour of Our Lady and of Saint Roc, with bullfights and firework displays.

Local arts and crafts feature works embroidered in Segovian point, glassworks and pottery. The local home-made sweets and pastries are also famed.

CUELLAR

Skirting enormous resin-producing pinewoods, we drive through towns and villages containing fine examples of brick Romanesque, such as Samboal, crossing the Eresma, Pirón and Cega river valleys until Cuéllar, 61 km from the capital, comes into view.

Cuéllar has many religious buildings, of which its churches form a unique, original whole. These are characterised by their high, square Romanesque towers, apse and, for the most part, Mudéjar brick portals. Their interiors are generally characterised by 17th- and 18th-century decoration, with gilt baroque altarpieces. Most are no longer used for worship, and several are privately-owned, but are being recovered by the autonomous government of Castile and León.

Descending from the castle esplanade to the Arévalo road we come across the following churches: **San Martín** (12th century); **San Andrés** (13th century); **Santiago** (12th century); **San Esteban** (12th century); and **San Miguel,** which presides over the Plaza Mayor. Of the **Church of Santa María** all that remains is the brick tower. Other religious buildings in Cuéllar are: the **Convent of La Trinidad;** the **Church of San Pedro; El Salvador; Santa María de la Cuesta;** the **Convent of La Concepción:** the **Convent of Santa Clara:** and the **Sanctuary of La Virgen del Henar.**

The **castle-palace** is the most outstanding civil monument in the town. Situated on the edge of a small meseta, at the highest point in Cuélla, its form suggests more an elegant palace than an austere fortress. It was ordered built in the 15th century by Beltrán de la Cueva.

Castle-palace, Cuéllar.

High altarpiece in the Church of San Juan Bautista (Carbonero el Mayor).

Walking through the streets of the town gives us the chance to admire some of its interesting houses. The centre is dotted with noble mansions and architectural beauty, with zig-zagging streets named after saints presiding over the parishes of the walls. The thresholds of the noble palaces are adorned with many escutcheons, and Cuéllar itself boasts a highly original motif: a beautiful horse's head.

The local fiesta is held on the last Sunday in August, with the renowned encierros, the oldest in Spain. In September, moreover, on the nearest Sunday to the 21, a *romería* takes place in honour of Our Lady of the Meadow.

CARBONERO EL MAYOR

The township huddles on one of the hillocks which spring up on the great plain between Cuéllar and Segovia. The most notable silhouette is that of the parish church. This is a friendly, lively town with an active economy and interesting reminders of its past. The origins of Carbonero el Mayor go back to the repopulation in the 12th and 13th centuries. Of the various religious buildings which once stood here, only the **Parish Church of San Juan Bautista** remains. Of simple lines, it has a huge dark brick tower with slate spire dating to the 17th century.

Carbonero el Mayor's other religious building is found some 4 km from the town in Los Nares. This is the **Hermitage of Nuestra Señora del Bustar,** the patron of which according to tradition, appeared to some local charcoal burners. The hermitage already existed in the 15th century, but the present building dates to 1780.

The civil buildings of Carbonero el Mayor are all finely-built. The most noteworthy is the **Palace of Los Avriales,** now owned by the local savings bank, with a lovely Renaissance gallery, and the Town Hall.

The fiestas of Carbonero el Mayor take the form of two romerias dedicated to the patron saint of the town. One is held on the Saturday before Pentecost, the other, which takes place on around 8 September, is the more important, with the dancing of jotas all the way to the hermitage, as well as other dances, such as the **paloteo** and the curious **danza de la cruz,** in which the dancers form the a cross inside the hermitage itself.

Local arts and crafts include the manufacture of dulcians, the Segovian musical instrument *par excellence,* to the sound of which are danced jotas and paloteos.

Dome of the Church of San Juan Bautista.

ITINERARY 5

Itinerary 5, with a length of some 230 km, combines sights of natural and historic interest. Amidst the fine scenery of the Sierra lie Navafría and Prádena, after which we come to such towns and villages of the meseta as Riaza, Ayllón and Maderuelo, all enriched by their historic links with Don Alvaro de Luna.

NAVAFRIA

This is a charming village 31 km from Segovia, surrounded by a huge green mass of pinewoods at the northern end of the Sierra de Guadarrama. Navafría is a typical town of the Sierra, and does not surprise us by possessing great religious and civil monuments, but does have three notable tourist attractions: the pinewood, its fiestas and its arts and crafts.
Navafría's pinewood is one of the loveliest in Europe and, without a doubt, the best-organised in Spain. It extends over a great mountainous range up to the heights of Nevero, where the River Cega is born, famous amongst fishermen for its trout. Take the turning 2 km outside the town on the road to Lozoya to reach the pinewood and the 27-hectare **El Chorro** recreational park, run by ICONA.

View of Navafría.

Cave of Los Enebralejos.

The second attraction of the town is the Feast of Saint Sebastian, held in honour of women, on 20 January. During it, four married women and four single, two of them children, all attired in the solemn traditional local costume, leave their houses to attend twelve o'clock mass.

Regarding arts and crafts, copper-work is still alive in Navafría, and a local craftsman still works with a martinete, a kind of hammer driven by water) producing charming copper pups which will delight the visitor.

PRADENA

Prádena lies amidst a forest of juniper and oak. It is important locally due to its wood industry and as a commercial centre. It is made up of great lintelled houses surrounding the elaborate, neoclassical church. This area is a veritable paradise for lovers of archaeology, caving and geology. Archaeological remains from various periods, particularly the Visigoth, have been found here, but the most spectacular find was the **Cave of Los Enebralejos,** situated on the outskirts of the village on the Casla road. This cave has three large chambers and galleries at various levels and is filled with extraordinarily-coloured stalactites and stalagmites. It was apparently inhabited during the Aeneolithic period.

Prádena celebrates Holy Week in highly emotive fashion, with the Calvary Procession on Good Friday as the most moving event. The statue of Christ Crucified is carried through the steep streets of the village on the shoulders of its bearers. There are no drums, or bands, or tourists. The deep-voiced men intone hymns whilst the women surround the Virgin of Solitude and the Virgin of Pity, this last a 15th-century Flemish Gothic statue.

Another of Prádena's attractions is its **textile mill**, where visitors can witness the manual production of high-quality materials for carpets, blankets and fine fabrics.

RIAZA

Riaza lies 87 km from the capital and is a town whose origins go back to the birth of the earldom of Castile, founded by Count Gonzalo Fernández around the year 1000. From 1139 to 1430, it was an ecclesiastical estate, later being purchased by King John II from the bishops of Segovia and finally came

Riaza: town hall and Plaza Mayor.

Riaza: parish church.

under the domain of Don Alvaro de Luna until the abolition of feuds in the 19th century.

Farming was always the main economic activity of Riaza, though mining and other industries flourished at one time or another. Now, the chief source of income is the service industry, as Riaza is the local market-town and an important tourist resort and summer retreat. The town's coat of arms features two trout and two waves, alluding to the richness of its rivers.

The parish church is dedicated to the **Virgin of the Mantle**, and is a Gothic building with Renaissance additions and reforms dating to the late-18th century. Its most notable works include an interesting high altarpiece, a 17th-century sculpture of the Pieta in the style of the Castilian school, and a wooden carving of Christ Recumbent in a glass urn.

The great noble houses, with their escutcheons and grilles form a pleasant whole, and include the Vélez de Guevara house, a 16th-century building with 17th-century baroque chapel. Nevertheless, the most interesting architectural element is that formed by Plaza Mayor.

The main fiesta in Riaza is held on the second Sunday in September in honour of the Virgin of Hontanares, with a romería to the 17th-century hermitage of the same name, including procession, popular dances, morning encierros and bullfighting in Plaza Mayor.

AYLLON

The town of Ayllón, 97 km from the capital, lies on the slopes of a reddish hill at whose peak stands an old military tower. Ayllón reached its period of maximum splendour during the Middle Ages.

Of the 13 parish churches it boasted in the 14th century, Ayllón now has only one active and the remains of four others. The **Church of San Miguel** is Romanesque in origin, with the Gothic and Plateresque tombs of local dignitaries. The **Church of San Juan,** which lies in a ruinous state, dates to the 12th century and is the oldest in the town. It features the Gothic-Renaissance Chapel of San Sebastián.

Of the **Church of San Martín** all that remains is the belltower, built over the tower, and which takes its name of **La Martina** from the advocation of the church itself. The **Church of San Nicolás** conserves only its fine Romanesque portal, which now provides access to the cemetery.

Ruins of the Convent of San Francisco de Asís.

«La Martina».

The **Church of Santa María la Mayor** is one which is still in active use. Backing onto Plaza Mayor, this is a Renaissance-style building with a huge belltower.

The convents of Ayllón include that of the Conceptionist nuns, with large Renaissance façade with the coats of arms of the Marquises of Villena, who founded the convent in 1546. Inside the church is a fine statue of the «Immaculate Conception» attributed to Alonso Cano.

The **Convent of San Francisco** lies without the town walls in a ruinous state. It was founded by Saint Francis himself and Prince Ferdinand of Antequera, regent king of Castile resided here for a time before becoming king of Aragon.

Ayllón conserves parts of its old city walls, including the paredones (thick adobe walls on the hill) and the beautiful

Gate in the city walls, Maderuelo.

Arco, or main entrance gate to the town. Opposite this is the Roman bridge over the River Aguisejo. Crossing under the **Arco,** we come to the splendid **Palace of Juan de Contreras,** built in 1497 in Elizabethan style according to the Gothic inscription on the front. The **Palace of Bishop Velosillo,** the **Aguila house** and the **House of Los Capellanes** are other interesting 16th-century buildings in Ayllón.

Plaza Mayor, with its arcades and old shops, contains the town hall, built in the 16th century and restored in 1804.

Various festivities take place each year in Ayllón; 5 February or the nearest Sunday is Saint Agatha's day, honouring women, and ending with hot chocolate for all early in the morning. Holy Week is celebrated with emotive processions, beginning on Palm Sunday and including Good Friday and Resurrection Sunday parades. Also important is the Fiesta of the Cross on the first Sunday in May, Mardi Gras before Carnival, and Carnival itself. Moreover, celebrations are also held in honour of the local patron saint, Michael, on 29 September. Local arts and crafts include articles made from woven rye straw.

MADERUELO

This history of Maderuelo differs little from that of other important towns and villages featuring in the different itineraries around the province. The village is perched 15 km from Ayllón on a fortified hill overlooking the waters of the Linares reservoir. It was repopulated by Count Fernán González and flourished particularly in the 13th century, when it had as many as ten parish churches.

The oldest religious monument in Maderuelo is the early-Romanesque **Hermitage of La Vera Cruz** which, like the Roman bridge, can be completely seen if the water level permits. This humble late-12th-century church was formerly decorated by Romanesque frescoes, now in the Prado Museum, Madrid.

The **Church of Santa María,** in the square, is a Romanesque building though later reformed. In a 15th-century chapel are Gothic tombs and a well-preserved mummy. The **Church of San Miguel** is another much-reformed but originally Romanesque building.

Generally speaking, the houses of Maderuelo are arranged in narrow streets with medieval old houses emblazoned with noble escutcheons and popular architecture with simple masonry, plaster and wood structures. The town has a walled section entered through the **gate,** with its battlemented towers. The arts and crafts of Maderuelo centre on leather accessories including suitcases, bags, wallets and purses and even riding saddles, all of the finest quality.

Linares: Roman bridge and Hermitage of La Vera Cruz.

ITINERARY 6

Itinerary 6 links spots in the area of pinewoods with deepest Castile, characterised by Romanesque works and such fortresses as those of Fuentidueña and Turégano. The 140 km covered by this route allow for breakfast in Fuentidueña and lunch in Turégano.

FUENTEPELAYO

This singular town, 38 km from the capital, lies on an extensive plain irrigated by the tiny Pirón and Malucas rivers. It boasts a spacious arcaded square containing the town hall and the **Parish Church of Santa María la Mayor.** The towers and apse of this church are Romanesque, and the main front overlooking the square, though deteriorated, is no less than one of those formerly pertaining to Segovia Cathedral, destroyed during the War of the Communities. Inside are magnificent Gothic ceilings, a fine Renaissance choir, a pulpit of carved limestone, and a statue of the Virgin of the Rosary and the **Altarpiece of the Quinta Angustia,** 16th-century works by Pedro Bolduque.

On the outskirts is the **Church of El Salvador,** originally Romanesque though now much altered. It has a lovely Mudéjar

Parish Church of Santa María la Mayor, Fuentepelayo.

Altarpiece of the «Quinta Angustia».

ceiling, an altar dedicated to Saint Peter, by Pedro Bolduque and a 16th-century cross by the Segovian silversmith Antonio de Oquendo.

The fiestas of Fuentepelayo take place on 2 and 3 February, day of Las Candelas, and at Corpus, when the famous stick dance known as the paloteo is performed in the church.

AGUILAFUENTE

Aguilafuente lies in an area of flat cereal fields and pinewoods. This venerable town of sloping-roofed houses has a charming, sunny main square, in which, besides the town hall, stands the impressive church with medieval tower over the crossing,

Romanesque brick apse and a south front in delicate late-Gothic style. Near to Aguilafuente, on the Turégano road, by the banks of the Cega were discovered during the 1970s the remains of a Roman road which formerly ran from Coca to Segovia, the ruins of a circus and fine mosaics from the Imperial period. Also unearthed was a Visigoth necropolis with fibulae, brooches, rings, lamps, necklaces, etc.

The 25 October is the Feast of the Holy Christ, with lively dancing and performances of popular jotas.

FUENTIDUEÑA

The village, lying at the foot of a hill surrounded by the ruins of various stretches of wall, has a timeless look. A walled city, it was once the capital of a Community of Town and Land pertaining, amongst other feudal lords, to Don Alvaro de Luna, who left his escutcheon on doors and walls.

View of Fuentidueña.

Romanesque Hermitage of the Virgen del Pinar, Cantalejo.

At the top of the village, overlooking the impressive gullies of the Duratón Valley, are the sad ruins of the Romanesque **Church of San Martín.** On the other side of the hill is, intact, the **Parish Church of San Miguel.** Its porticoed gallery is, unusually on the north side, facing the village, and is clearly influenced by Cistercian art. The building has a single nave and is presided over by a carved statue of the Archangel Michael. The baroque altars also feature interesting carvings, including a Renaissance crucifix.

Impressive, though somewhat deteriorated civil buildings include the Palace of Los Luna and that of the Count of Montijo. Plaza Mayor is a charming square featuring delicate popular architecture, with arcades and long wooden balconies. Before leaving Fuentidueña, we can stop to buy fine *hogazas,* cottage loaves, famous throughout the province.

CANTALEJO

Standing in lands of pinewoods and cereal fields some 50 km from Segovia, Cantalejo is one of the largest villages in the province, characterised by the ingeniousness of its industrious inhabitants. Here are sawmills, potters' kilns, mosaic factories, flour mills, farms, etc. Cantalejo has always been famed for its wood and flint threshing machines, which used to be sold all over Spain.

In the late-18th century a colony of French immigrants arrived in Cantalejo, fleeing the French Revolution. They traded in animals, particularly horses, and in farming utensils.

The Parish Church of Cantalejo is dedicated to Saint Andrew and is a neoclassical building dating to the 17th century. It has a nave and two aisles and boasts a sumptuous altarpiece with marble columns. Two km from the village is the Romanesque Hermitage of La Virgen del Pilar, built by the Knights Templar and greatly reformed in the 19th century.

This flourishing village celebrates various feasts during the course of the year. Particularly emotive are those of Las Candelas on 2 and 3 February, and the *romería* the Virgin of the Pillar on Pentecost Monday. The arts and crafts of Cantalejo offer traditional farming tools (threshers, sieves, corn measures) and excellent *botas* for wine.

Turégano.

Turégano: the castle.

TUREGANO

The village of Turégano lies some 34 km from Segovia. Its narrow, winding streets, flanked by typical buildings, have a markedly medieval air. The Plaza Mayor and the unusual castle give the village a character all its own,and it has been repeatedly portrayed by painters such as Ignacio Zuloaga or the photographer Ortiz de Echagüe.

The **Parish Church of Santiago** stands in the little square adjoining Plaza Mayor. Of its original Romanesque fabric it conserves the apse, sandwiched between later elements. Inside is an interesting high altar, baroque in style, with sculptures of Saint Peter and Saint Paul.

The **castle,** situated on a gentle hill in the north of the village is an unusual example of the church-fortress which has intrigued amateurs and art scholars alike. With a rectangular ground plan, cylindrical turrets and massive, heavy main body crowned by a great three-storey baroque belltower, the castle

Gothic Parish Church of San Abdón y San Senén, Cantimpalos.

is built from strange ochre and pink coloured stone. The original nucleus of the castle is formed by a Romanesque church dating to the 12th and 13th centuries, over which was built the fortress we now admire. The church is dedicated to Saint Michael, whose image presides over the high altar. In Holy Week, on Good Friday, an unusual procession takes place here.

Other important festivities in Turégano, though of a very different nature, are the medieval fiestas which take place on the first Sunday after 8 September and feature **encierros,** traditional bullfighting in Plaza Mayor and the **toro de fuego.** Lovers of antiques will be delighted to browse in the local shops, selling a great variety of ancient objects.

CANTIMPALOS

Some 20 km from Segovia, Cantimpalos lies in the heart of the country, though bordering on the foothills of the Sierra. The village flourished in the 15th and, particularly, the 16th centuries, enjoying the period of splendour which affected the entire district and which was based on agriculture, highly profitable in those days, though local farming is now much more concerned with livestock.

The Parish Church of San Abdón y San Senén is dedicated to Our Lady of the Immaculate Conception and is late-Gothic in style, dating back to the mid-16th century. The church is of the single-chapel type, with a stone vault, body of nave and two aisles covered with wood, and a baroque altarpiece at the head.

Lively festivities are celebrated in Cantimpalos in honour of the Virgin, with exhibitions of jotas and paloteo. As regards gastronomy, the sausages of Cantimpalos are a great delicacy, particularly the **chorizo de Cantimpalos.**

Detail of the high altarpiece, with Our Lady of the Immaculate Conception (patron saint of Cantimpalos).

ITINERARY 7

Itinerary 7 takes us to a great variety of small villages and important towns, following the old routes through canyons and the Tejadilla Valley. Our tour will take us over some 150 km, but the return trip to Segovia along the Avila road offers the attraction of viewing the Fuentemilanos aerodrome.

MELQUE

Melque, originally Melic, a Mozarabic name, is situated half-way between Santa María la Real de Nieva and Martín Muñoz de las Posadas, some 37 km from Segovia. The principal attraction of the village is the **old church,** until recently used as a cemetery. It is situated at the northwest end of the village and is one of the finest existing examples of 12th- and early-13th-century Romanesque brick works. It was restored recently and an excellent brick portal was uncovered, the wall having been covered and painted for use in the game of pelota, very popular in this area.

Restored brick doorway in the old church.

Parish Church, Martín Muñoz de las Posadas.

MARTIN MUÑOZ DE LAS POSADAS

The Segovian historian Diego de Colmenares says that this village was founded by a knight from Burgos towards the end of the 12th century, and who gave his name to it. What is undoubtedly true is the King Alphonse X, the Wise, incorporated it into Segovia province, in 1358 confirming its dependence on the Council of Segovia.

The importance of the village lies in the fact that it was the birthplace, in 1505, of Don Diego de Espinosa, general inquisitor, president of the Council of Castile and cardinal of the Holy Church of Rome.

The **parish church,** a late-Gothic edifice dating to the mid-16th century, has an altarpiece made in 1584 featuring panels by Antonio Martín and Mateo Imberto, and two works of exceptional importance: the alabaster tomb of the cardinal, by

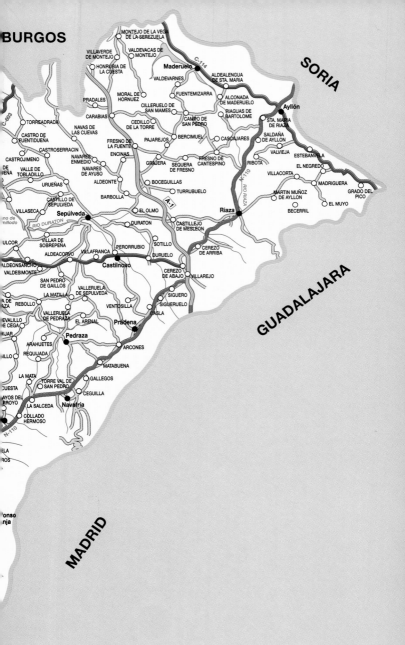

BURGOS

SORIA

GUADALAJARA

MADRID

MONTEJO DE LA VEGA
DE LA SEREZUELA

VILLAVERDE
DE MONTEJO
VALDEVACAS DE
MONTEJO
Maderuelo
C-114
ALDEALENGUA
DE STA. MARIA
HONRUBIA DE
LA CUESTA
VALDEVARNES
PRADALES
MORAL DE
HORNUEZ
FUENTEMIZARRA
ALCONADA
DE MADERUELO
Ayllón
CARABIAS
CILLERUELO DE
SAN MAMES
RIAGUAS DE
BARTOLOME
STA. MARIA
DE RIAZA
TORREADRADA
NAVAS DE
LAS CUEVAS
CEDILLO
DE LA TORRE
CAMPO DE
SAN PEDRO
C-603
CASTRO DE
FUENTIDUEÑA
FRESNO DE
LA FUENTE
PAJAREJOS
BERCIMUEL
CASCAJARES
SALDAÑA
DE AYLLON
CASTROSERRACIN
ENCINAS
VALVIEJA
ESTEBANVELA
CASTROJIMENO
NAVARES
ENMEDIO
GRAJERA
FRESNO DE
CANTESPINO
RIBOTA
EL NEGREDO
DE
ENA
VALLE DE
TOBLADILLO
NAVARES
DE AYUSO
SEQUERA
DE FRESNO
VILLACORTA
MADRIGUERA
URUEÑAS
ALDEONTE
MARTIN MUÑOZ
DE AYLLON
GRADO DEL
PICO
CASTILLO DE
SEPULVEDA
BARBOLLA
BOCEGUILLAS
TURRUBUELO
EL MUYO
VILLASECA
no de
nillodo
EL OLMO
BECERRIL
Sepúlveda
RIO DURATON
DURATON
CASTILLEJO
DE MESLEON
Riaza
ULCOR
VILLAR DE
SOBREPEÑA
PERORRUBIO
SOTILLO
CEREZO
DE ARRIBA
ALDEONSANCHO
ALDEACORVO
VILLAFRANCA
DURUELO
VALDESIMONTE
Castilnovo
CEREZO
DE ABAJO
VILLAREJO
SAN PEDRO
DE GAILLOS
VALLERUELA
DE SEPULVEDA
SIGUERO
A DE
ZA
LA MATILLA
REBOLLO
VENTOSILLA
SIGUERUELO
EVALILLO
E CEGA
VALLERUELA
DE PEDRAZA
EL ARENAL
CASLA
Prádena
IJAR
Pedraza
ARAHUETES
ARCONES
REQUIJADA
ILLO
MATABUENA
LA MATA
TORRE VAL DE
SAN PEDRO
GALLEGOS
CUESTA
CEGUILLA
AYOS DEL
RROYO
LA SALCEDA
Navafría
N-110
COLLADO
HERMOSO
ELA
ROS
RIO RIAZA
N-110
A-1
onso
nja

Pompeyo Leoni in around 1582, and a painting by El Greco representing «The Crucified, the Virgin and Saint John», along with a personage from the time of the painting, Don Andrés Muñoz, priest of the Church of Santo Tomé in Toledo.

Plaza Mayor is a wide square, its south side lined by arcades. The town hall, a Renaissance building, stands on the corner whilst close by stands the magnificent **Palace of Cardinal Espinosa.** This is a building dating to 1572, in brick and stone, with two turrets at either end, crowned by slate spires, and a front with classicist-style columns featuring the royal coat of arms and the escutcheon of the builder. The palace has a majestic Plateresque courtyard and a graceful staircase. Its design is attributed to Juan Bautista of Toledo, prime artifice of the Monastery of El Escorial.

Tomb of Cardinal Diego de Espinosa.

Church of San Sebastián, Villacastín.

VILLACASTIN

Villacastín lies in a small valley in the northern slopes of the Sierra de Guadarrama, half on the hill and half on the plain. The district is irrigated by four streams, the Piedga, the Tijeras, the Viejas and that of El Valle, all of which flow into the River Moros. During the Middle Ages, this was a village forming part of the Lands of Segovia, until Philip IV granted it its town charter.

The town's most interesting monument is the enormous parish church, a grey granite building dedicated to Saint Sebastian. It is isolated from the houses of the town, and its construction is generally considered to have been commenced in 1529.

Other religious buildings in the outskirts are also worth mentioning. The **Hermitage of Nuestra Señora del Carrascal,** a 15th-century building, stands on a hill, its advocation due to a legendary apparition of the Virgin over a bush known as a carrascal. The entire building is painted with works by Francisco Gutiérrez in 1651. The other hermitage, situated in a spot known as «el valle», the valley, is dedicated to **El Santísimo Cristo,** but is also known as the Hermitage of El Valle. This has a magnificent Morisco wooden ceiling. The streets of the town are filled with houses emblazoned with coats of arms, whilst Plaza Mayor is an arcaded square, and the town hall, with clocktower, form a typical picture of a Segovian town.

In May, the romería of the Virgen del Carrascal takes place, whilst, turning to arts and crafts, the embroidery of the Villacastín area is rightly famed.

High altarpiece in the Church of San Sebastián.

Parish Church, El Espinar.

EL ESPINAR

Twenty-two km from Villacastín is El Espinar, lying in the foothills of the Sierra de Guadarrama on a small hill taking the shape of an amphitheatre surrounded by mountains. This picturesque village was officially founded by the Community and Land of Segovia which in 1297 gave it its charter, placing it «in an uninhabited place to the south of the capital». On the present site of El Espinar in around the year 1210 King Henry I built a hunting lodge, which became known in the 14th century as the **Palace,** and of which today all that remains are some ruins on the outskirts of the town. In 1626, Philip IV gave it the status of town, ever since when it has been independent of the jurisdiction of Segovia.

The parish church is dedicated to Saint Euthropy due, according to legend, appeared miraculously to a little shepherd-girl. The building is a magnificent example of mid-16th-century architecture, constructed over the site of an earlier church destroyed by fire in 1542. It has a basilical ground plan, with Gothic groined vaults and an 18th-century bevelled sacristy. Inside is a fine altarpiece, built in 1565 by the artist Francisco Giralte.

Another interesting religious building is the **Sanctuary of El Cristo del Caloco,** where a lively romería takes place each 14 September. The local festivities take place on 16 August in honour of the patron saint of the town, Saint Roc.

Hermitage of San Antonio del Cerro.

NAVAS DE SAN ANTONIO

Situated on gentle slopes close to the CN-VI road, the town spreads out extensively, seeming larger than it really is. The poor, stony ground on which it stands contains quarries from which is extracted stone good for building and which went to help construct the **Parish Church of San Nicolás,** aloof in a spacious square, dominating the rest of the town due to its impressively strong structure. This is a building of simple design, dating to the late-15th and early-16th centuries, with crossing vaults and terceletes, their keys decorated with splendid figures.

But the chief attraction of Navas de San Antonio is its hermitage, 4 km outside the village, and known as that of **San Antonio del Cerro** due to the apparition of Saint Anthony on the hill in 1455. The *romería* in honour of the saint takes place each 13 June, bringing together people from all around, many in fulfillment of a promise.

VEGAS DE MATUTE

This is a tiny village lying on the slopes of Guadarrama, on rocky ground of little agricultural worth, its main source of income traditionally livestock farming, particularly sheep farming. The origins of the village are thought to be noble, and its development was always linked to the house owned locally by the Segovia family.

The **Parish Church** of Vegas de Matute is an outstanding stone building with two unequal naves. The difference, appreciable both in the exterior and the interior, is due to the fact that the church was built in different stages.

The origin of the church is a small chapel dedicated to Saint Thomas, built by a member of the Segovia family during the first half of the 16th century. Its original purpose was as the burial-place of the family, and it was designed by Rodrigo Gil de Hontañón. The keys of the vault groins feature reliefs of Saint Peter, Saint Paul and Saint Thomas. After 1582, a new construction was added on the north side, adjoining the chapel, resulting in the present Church of San Pedro. Inside is an altarpiece attributed to Berruguete, and a painting attributed to Zurbarán.

Environs of Vegas de Matute.

CONTENTS

The printing of this book was completed
in the workshops of
FISA - ESCUDO DE ORO, S.A.
Palaudarias, 26 - Barcelona (Spain)